WORKS BY ANDREW WYETH

This catalogue was made possible by a grant from the Metropolitan Life Foundation

Cover illustration: THE QUAKER, 1975
Egg tempera on panel, 36¾ x 40⅜ in.

WORKS BY ANDREW WYETH

FROM THE

HOLLY AND ARTHUR MAGILL COLLECTION

ON LOAN TO

THE GREENVILLE COUNTY MUSEUM OF ART

ISBN 09603246-0-7 Case Bound
ISBN 0-9603246-1-5 Paper
ISBN 0-9603246-2-3 Leather
LC 79-53937

First Printing, 1979
Printed in the United States of America

CONTENTS

PREFACE

X

On 19 March 1979 the American art world was stunned to learn that Holly and Arthur Magill of Greenville, South Carolina, had acquired Mr. and Mrs. Joseph E. Levine's renowned collection of paintings by Andrew Wyeth with the expressed intent that it would become a gift to the Greenville County Museum of Art.

The following day in a front page story, *New York Times* art critic Grace Glueck described the acquisition's impact on "a little-known museum in Greenville, S.C." and in an Associated Press release John Canaday (author of the accompanying essay in this catalogue) explained that "a hitherto obscure museum in a small Southern city took the art world by surprise." Subsequent articles in newspapers and periodicals throughout the country carried the message until Sally Devaney, in a feature story for the *ART gallery Magazine*, proclaimed such critical appellations as "little-known" and "obscure" were "a thing of the past for the Greenville County Museum of Art."

The story actually began five years earlier when on 9 March 1974 the Greenville County Museum of Art opened the doors of its new facilities on Heritage Green in downtown Greenville. Construction for the modern four-level structure had been financed by an unprecedented contribution from the Magills and a county-wide bond issue.

To complement a small but impressive permanent collection of contemporary American art the Museum was opened to the public with a major restrospective exhibition of 106 works by the renowned illustrator N.C. Wyeth. The success of *N.C. Wyeth* led to plans for a survey of work by other Brandywine artists. *Andrew Wyeth in Southern Collections* drew record attendance in 1978 and *Artists of the Brandywine: Howard Pyle and his Students* was presented in 1979. These efforts to acquaint the Piedmont region with the Brandywine tradition had established and strengthened ties with similar projects at the Brandywine River Museum in Chadds Ford, Pennsylvania and the Delaware Museum of Art in Wilmington, Delaware. Most important, perhaps, was the cooperation of the Wyeth family and their representatives Fred Woolworth of E. Coe Kerr Gallery, New York City, and Frank Fowler of Lookout Mountain, Tennessee. Mr. Fowler has been especially instrumental in the recent growth and development of the Museum's permanent collection.

On Thursday, 1 March 1979 the Magills learned that Mr. and Mrs. Joseph E. Levine's internationally known collection of paintings by Andrew Wyeth was about to be placed on the market. Moving quickly and decisively with the assistance of Frank Fowler and Fred Woolworth, Holly and Arthur Magill acquired the Levine Collection two weeks later.

From *Rum Runner*, originally entitled *To The Westward*, which was completed in 1944 (only to be repainted and renamed after damage in 1974) to the *Kass* completed in 1978, the eight temperas, twelve watercolors and six dry-brush paintings represent a full range of Wyeth's work to date. Many of the pieces are already familiar images through reproductions that hang in homes and public places across the country, while others are coming to public attention for the first time. Chadds Ford, Pennsylvania and Cushing, Maine, Kuerners and Olsons, and "interest in people as human beings" and an "emotional response to the countryside" as Canaday has written, are all represented in this collection. Most important, however, is the opportunity offered here for careful and extended study of an infinitely complex and subtle talent. As Thomas Hoving has written in his foreword for *Two Worlds of Andrew Wyeth: Kuerners and Olsons*, "the perception of subtlety and complexity is the immediate progenitor of contemplation and knowledge."

With the Magill announcement adjectives were quickly depleted by critics and reporters; atlases across America were consulted for the location of Greenville, South Carolina. The Wyeth Phenomenon, as it has often been described, had once more taken hold of the public's imagination. That twenty-six paintings by America's best known artist could generate such a response was not unusual. That such a complete selection of Andrew Wyeth's work had been assembled over a ten year period and changed hands intact was, however, unique.

An event of this magnitude is not without the supporting efforts of a highly trained professional staff: John Petty, Chief Conservator, Southeastern Regional Conservation Center who examined and prepared the works for exhibition; Sylvia Marchant, Director of Education; Allison Muller, Curator; Claudia Beckwith, Registrar, who researched and compiled material for this catalogue; Tamara Noble, Director of Public Information, for critical reading of the text; Stephen Dell, Associate Curator, and Michael McDunn, Woodcraftsman who designed and installed the exhibition; Blake Praytor, Director of Electra-graphics, whose exceptional design expertise and photography is evident throughout this publication; and Caryl Palmer, Administrative Assistant, who typed and compiled endless pages of copy.

We are especially grateful to Betsy Wyeth and Mary Adam Gale for their generous cooperation and assistance and to Andrew Wyeth who graciously provided original source material on each work for this publication.

Jack A. Morris, Jr.
Executive Director

INTRODUCTION

ANDREW WYETH, CHADDS FORD, 1976

Arnold Newman

14

In commenting on the Holly and Arthur Magill collection of works by Andrew Wyeth, a critic may rest comfortably in the knowledge that no matter what he says, or fails to say, or discovers or bungles in the saying, the pictures will continue to speak for themselves to an enormous audience ranging from people who know nothing about art to the most demanding collectors. The word "pictures" in that sentence is important and is used deliberately instead of "paintings," which is ordinarily preferred. "Paintings" not only covers everything from total abstraction to hyper-realism, but also implies that the interest of a work of art lies not in its subject matter — what it is "about" — but in technique, esthetic effect, and philosophical content, while "pictures" implies, with faintly derogatory associations, that the first interest is in subject matter for its own sake, with some sacrifice of creative values.

Andrew Wyeth's art is an exception to the rule that does not prove it but simply contradicts it in a way unique to a major twentieth-century painter who is also one of the major picture-makers of any century. His technical mastery is superb; he obviously enjoys tremendously the mere physical act of painting, as all great technicians do, but unlike them, whether realists or abstract "action painters," Wyeth never seeks to amaze by technical display. His absolute control of his medium is always directed toward an expressive (or call it philosophical) goal, and every stroke of the brush in his meticulously detailed representations of his subjects — his picturizations — is directed toward that goal.

Contradictions are inescapable in any consideration of Andrew Wyeth. Here is a painter working traditionally in a century when the excitement of radical innovations in one form or another, following one another in succession like a string of firecrackers fused by Matisse and Picasso, has become art's primary and imperative characteristic. Our post-World War II continuation of the great days of the revolution of modern art has maintained this excitement by esthetic, intellectual, and commerical collaboration between artists, critics, and dealers, who have stimulated a continuous battle of styles — abstract expressionism, minimal art, op art, pop art, conceptual art, and photo-realism among them. Wyeth, virtually alone among major artists, has stood aside from such developments.

Yet in his isolation Wyeth has become not only the best known American painter in his own country but also the most widely honored American internationally, with Tokyo, Moscow, Paris, and London among his official conquests. At a time when sales at high prices are accepted as proof of the validity of this or that new movement, Wyeth has become, by a natural process of supply and demand, the highest priced living painter in this or any other country. Prices, of course, are an unworthy standard of measure; nevertheless, it pleases Wyeth's admirers when his supremacy in the marketplace hoists his detractors with their own petard — for detractors he has had among the tastemakers.

By an odd quirk of contemporary art history, traditional values have to be defended today against fashionable novelties just as creative innovation had to be defended against academic ossification earlier in this century and in the late nineteenth. But there is not much point in pitting Wyeth against the field in a debate that has become wearisome. There is more to be learned by trying to explain why he alone among painters who can be called traditionally realists has become a major artist, why he is just as isolated from the conservative rank and file as he is from the radical horde. Dozens, perhaps hundreds, of proficient realists have adopted the Wyeth iconography of weathered houses, stubbled fields, the paraphernalia of country life from small boats and wagons to battered buckets and, for the most skillful borrowers, the faces of country people arresting in their plainness but — when Wyeth paints them — impressive in their dignity. A compendium of Wyeth's favorite motifs could be culled from the Magill pictures alone, which also offer multiple examples of Wyeth's four most persistent themes: farm buildings of stone or wood set in the bare countryside, such as the classic *Weather Side* (#24); spare, immaculate interiors of these same houses (*The Quaker*, #4); complicated still lifes — for that is what they amount to — of homely objects like those in *Hay Ledge* (#26); and psychological portraits like the wonderful *Buzzard's Glory* (#9).

Wyeth's hopeful followers have treated subjects like these picturesquely, from the outside only, capitalizing on their element of quaint appeal just as, in the nineteenth century, scenes of the simple life were fabricated by fashionable painters for an urban audience, neither painter nor audience having any personal emotional associations with the subjects. The thing about Wyeth is that he is an extremely personal painter. He paints places, things, and people not as a detached observer but as a participant in a world he was not born into but has chosen to share. If he sometimes seems to share it in the role of lord of the manor, it is because he was born to that role and cannot always abandon it without admitting into his happy relationship with his friends a taint of falsity or condescension. Their lives are inextricably intertwined with his own and his family's. A vivid example is his friendship with Christina Olson, the crippled girl in his most famous painting, *Christina's World*, in the Museum of Modern Art, which was painted in 1948. Over a period of nearly thirty years until her [recent] death in 1968, Wyeth painted a series of portraits of Christina in which intimate poignance never for a moment lapses into sentimentality. *Weather Side* is one of Wyeth's several pictures of the Olsons' house.

The question has to be, of course, how Wyeth's powerful subjective associations with his material affect his presentation of subjects that in any analyzable terms remain meticulous objective reproductions of surfaces. The answer can only be that the transformation from the merely picturesque to the expressive, from surface reflection to the inner

meaning, is there. Wyeth said in a recent interview that his struggle as an artist is to "get to the bottom of reality," not to get a perfect imitation but to get "something that says how I feel."

However he does it (and he himself cannot explain it), Wyeth paints his response into his pictures; the emotional appeal that his art holds for his enormous public is a matter of his capacity to relay personal responses that affect him profoundly. A familiar definition of the function of art is "to clarify, intensify, or enlarge our experience of life." Whatever associations we already have with subjects similar to Wyeth's, his art clarifies, intensifies, or enlarges those associations by bringing them into focus through his own vision of otherwise unexceptional material.

That is why *Weather Side* becomes a place we know; why *The Quaker*, an empty room we have never seen, is haunted by the presence of people we have never known but seem to remember in it; why *Hay Ledge* evokes a spot we might have explored in childhood, whether or not we have ever been inside a barn, and why *Buzzard's Glory*, instead of offering us only a factual record of a set of undistinguished features belonging to a stranger, brings us into the presence of a living person to whom we respond with immediate understanding.

What all this comes down to is that, while the typical twentieth-century artist thinks of his work as a demonstration of theoretical principles offered for discussion with a band of specialists, Wyeth, this extremely personal artist, thinks of his pictures as a form of emotional communication with people in general — a goal that, after all, is his strongest tie to tradition in an age of revolution.

John Canaday

PLATES

1. CIDER BARREL
1968. Drybrush watercolor on paper.
22 x 29 in. (55.9 x 73.6 cm.)

A cider barrel rests on an old wagon behind the Wyeth home in Chadds Ford, a restored house at Brinton's Mill. Karl Kuerner used to make cider every year but "... how he made it died with him."

2. CANADA
1974. Watercolor on paper.
18 x 29 in. (45.7 x 73.7 cm.)

"Each winter morning my wife throws corn out for the flock of Canada geese that spend the cold months on the open water below our mill dam. One day she heard a shot. The panicked geese took off, but one died an hour later in her arms. She placed it in a basket which hung from a rafter in our open shed...she put it up there for me to bury. It was one of those things that just happened."

21

3. STUDY FOR THE IDES OF MARCH
ca. 1975. Watercolor and pencil on paper.
14¾ x 23¾ in. (37.5 x 60.4 cm.)

Wyeth's hound, Nell Gwyn, rests by the hearth,
eyes slightly open. "There's a strange mood of
quietness...something is about to happen. It's
just an expression in her eyes."

4. THE QUAKER
1975. Egg tempera on panel.
36¾ x 40⅜ in. (93.3 x 102.6 cm.)

Wyeth likes contrasts — the bitter cold visible through the window and the general feeling of the interior warmth of his studio fireplace; the glow of the sunlight reflected on the floor and the glaring brightness of the light reflected on the snow outside; two coats, one simple, sturdy — a Quaker coat — shows us its back, the other more elegant, of silk brocade is facing outward, open. "That's a Quaker coat that actually came from Lancaster, the dark coat, which is very simple and made of homespun weave. The other one probably was made in France and sent over for some American."

Two coats, passed down from Howard Pyle to N.C. Wyeth, are said to represent two sides of Wyeth's nature.

5. TOM'S SHED
1960. Watercolor on paper.
14 x 19⅞ in. (35.6 x 50.5 cm.)

Tom Clark, supposedly descended from the
Moors of Delaware, was a lean, majestic man
with great dignity, whose family was well ac-
quainted with the Wyeth household. His brother
worked for N. C. Wyeth for many years. Tom, the
subject of at least a dozen major works by
Wyeth, had a house that sat close to the rail-
road in Chadds Ford. His storage shed reflected
the personality and bearing of a good friend. "It
had a strange elegant quality about it even though
it was just an old shed. It wasn't just a building
to me. The long shadows on the shed wall re-
minded me of this tall, elegant man. His dignity
was king-like."

6. NOGEESHIK
  1972. Egg tempera on panel.
  24⅝ x 21¹⁵⁄₁₆ in. (62.5 x 55.7 cm.)

Nogeeshik, an Obijwa Indian from the Algonquin tribe, appeared abruptly on the Wyeths' doorstep in Pennsylvania one winter evening, with snowflakes falling on his long black hair and shoulders. Wyeth, struck by the intensity of the traveler persuaded him, a year later, to pose. "...he sat totally still but his piercing eyes had a way of looking right through me to something beyond. This remoteness and suppressed wildness endured to the end."

7. PETER WYETH HURD
1961. Drybrush watercolor and pencil on paper.
18 x 23¼ in. (45.7 x 59.1 cm.)

Peter Wyeth Hurd, Andrew Wyeth's nephew, is an accomplished pianist interested in ancient music and musical instruments. "I was anxious to catch the intensity of his profile as I had seen it so often when he played the piano, and also to express the quality of touch as his long fingers moved rapidly over the keys."

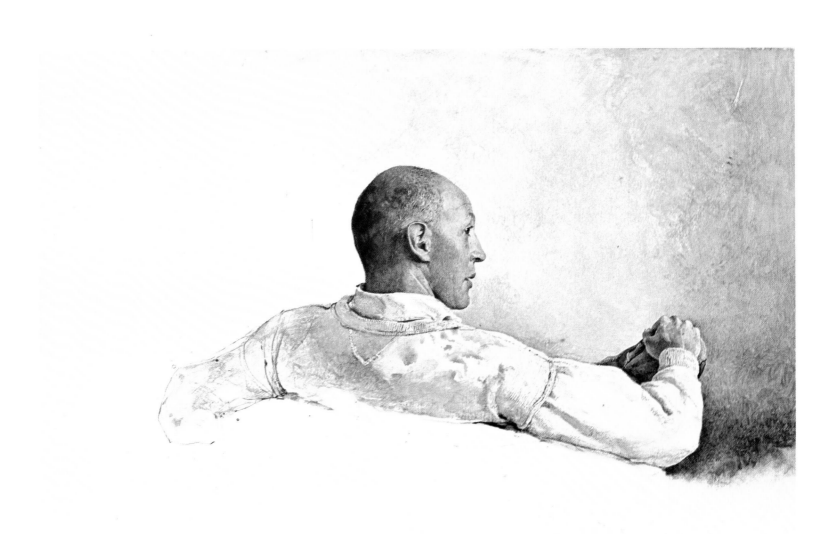

8. FROM THE CAPES
1974. Egg tempera on panel.
24¼ x 18⅝ in. (61.6 x 47.3 cm.)

Wyeth first painted Dr. Margaret Handy in 1949; the work was a more controlled portrait of his son's pediatrician entitled *Children's Doctor.* Now a close, personal friend of the family, Dr. Handy's Virginia heritage surfaces in this second portrait. "Her lineage included the father of Pocahontas, and the fiery orator Patrick Henry, which accounted for her high cheekbones and red hair. As a child she loved to roam the beaches of Rehoboth, Delaware and climb the Cape Henlopen Lighthouse which guided the ships entering Delaware Bay. One morning she had her hair down, loose...and I saw that hidden wildness with a touch of witchcraft and thought of her as a young girl off the capes with her long red hair blowing in the wind."

9. BUZZARD'S GLORY
1968. Egg tempera on panel.
18½ x 23⅞ in. (47 x 60.6 cm.)

The Lynch family lived along a stretch of road in Chadds Ford called Buzzard's Glory. The tale goes that the Lynches would shoot buzzards as they circled the marshes, and serve them for Sunday dinner.

Andrew Wyeth has painted the Lynch boys many times. Johnny Lynch, with his black hair and particular tilt to his eyes is a typical Lynch. Johnny has become very successful: "...he runs a business of building fences and has a lot of men working under him."

10. RAIN CLOUDS
1969. Watercolor on paper.
30¾ x 22¹⁄₁₆ in. (78.1 x 56 cm.)

"Jimmy Lynch stood looking at the heavy clouds like a young impatient Charles Lindbergh waiting for the skies to clear for a flight over the distant horizon."

Johnny Lynch and Jimmy are half brothers, with very different, distinct personalities. Jimmy is "much more uninhibited than Johnny."

11. THE SWINGER
1969. Drybrush watercolor on paper.
15⅜ x 25¹¹⁄₁₆ in. (39.1 x 65.2 cm.) image

Jimmy Lynch, a close friend of Wyeth's sons,
likes to sit on his front porch and watch the
girls go by.

12. THE KASS
1978. Watercolor on paper.
22⅞ x 28⅞ in. (58.1 x 73.4 cm.)

Wyeth has been painting Karl and Anna Kuerner
and their farm in Pennsylvania since 1932. These
images often reflect the solidity and strength of
Karl Kuerner's German background. "If objects
can become a portrait this watercolor repre-
sents my friend Karl Kuerner...the wardrobe
called the Kass, the German helmet he wore as
a machine gunner in the first World War, the
gun and my hound Nell, sleeping in the morning sun..."

13. KITCHEN GARDEN
1962. Drybrush watercolor on paper.
23½ x 22¼ in. (59.7 x 56.5 cm.)

The contrast between Karl and Anna Kuerner
is revealed in this intimate, snow-covered view
of the Kuerners farm. Karl, the sturdy outdoors-
man is reflected in the fields adjacent to the
frozen pond, and Anna Kuerner's garden, just
outside the kitchen door, reveals the introverted,
aloof Anna and her home-oriented work. "This
was one of those covered glass little gardens
where they would grow early lettuce, things
like that — celery."

43

14. FENCE LINE
   1967. Watercolor on paper.
   21⅞ x 30 in. (55.6 x 76.2 cm.)

Approaching the Kuerner house from the back,
the snowswept hills reflect the bleak, cold Pennsylvania winter. "I prefer winter and fall, when
you feel the bone structure in the landscape —
the loneliness of it — the dead feeling of winter.
Something waits beneath it — the whole story
doesn't show."

45

15. LODEN COAT
1978. Watercolor on paper.
30 x 22 in. (76.2 x 55.9 cm.)

Karl Kuerner's final illness occurred in mid-winter. His German nurse would walk down his driveway toward the house in her Loden coat every morning at exactly the same hour. "The German precision endured even though he was bedridden."

47

16. RUM RUNNER (STUDY OF
WALTER ANDERSON)
1974. Watercolor on paper.
15 x 8 in. (38.1 x 20.3 cm.)

17. RUM RUNNER
1944-1974. Egg tempera on panel.
25 x 48 in. (63.5 x 121.9 cm.)

The Wyeths had their first summer home at Port
Clyde, Maine, where Wyeth met Walter Anderson, when Anderson was but five years old. A
man of varied talents, including poaching for
lobsters, Wyeth chose his friend to model for
this mystical sea scene because "....underneath
you feel the pirate side to his personality. There
is something mysterious about a sail appearing
suddenly from nowhere and passing swiftly by
an island that reminds me of treachery at sea...
underneath his charm was a real pirate."

51

18. SEA SNAILS
1953. Watercolor on paper.
20 x 28⅛ in. (50.8 x 71.4 cm.)

"When the tide goes out below my studio in
Maine these two boulders sit like two encrusted
sea crowns covered with snails and barnacles."

53

19. TEEL'S ISLAND
1954. Drybrush watercolor on paper.
10 x 23 in. (25.4 x 58.4 cm.)

Henry Teel lived on an island, alone, near Port
Clyde, Maine. Although he and Wyeth were close
friends he would not pose. In the fall of 1974
Henry Teel returned to the mainland to be near
his doctor, for he was dying of cancer. Fearing
that his friend would be gone the following
spring, Wyeth visited the island, and the loneliness of his friend's skiff hauled up above high
water prompted this drybush watercolor.

20. ELWELL'S SAWMILL
1968. Watercolor on paper.
22$\frac{1}{16}$ x 30$\frac{5}{8}$ in. (56 x 77.8 cm.)

Old man Elwell has gone his way alone, with his
primitive tools and team of horses, and has
operated a one-man sawmill in a valley near
Cushing throughout his lifetime.

57

21. LOGGING SCOOT
1968. Watercolor on paper.
22 x 30½ in. (55.9 x 77.5 cm.)

Every day Elwell followed the same routine:
drive the team to the mill, fell a few trees along
his woods road, walk back and hitch the team
to a scoot, and haul logs back to his mill. He had
watched his trees grow, and now he hoped to
cut them all before he died.

22. SPRUCE BOUGH
1969. Watercolor on paper.
21¾ x 29¹⁵⁄₁₆ in. (55.2 x 76 cm.)

A snowstorm came early in Cushing — the twenty-second of October. The spruce trees were heavy with snow that transformed this small detail of nature.

23. THE FINN
1969. Drybrush watercolor on paper.
29¾ x 21½ in. (75.5 x 54.6 cm.)

The Finnish people, strong and self-reliant, have settled in and around Cushing, Maine. Wyeth has painted George Erickson's daughter, Siri, several times. One day he captured George in his shed doorway. "I'd go by and see him standing in the door with that amazing oval head, very brown, burned by the sun and eyes squinting."

24. WEATHER SIDE
1965. Egg tempera on panel.
48⅛ x 27⅞ in. (122.2 x 70.8 cm.)

"It's a portrait...a portrait I call that picture, really." *Weather Side* is the summation of an emotional and artistic relationship that spanned twenty-five years. A portrait of a house, a farm in Maine, and inside it, next to it, and at each window, a portrait of Anna Christina and Alvaro Olson.

25. CHRISTINA'S TEAPOT
1968. Watercolor on paper.
23 x 28$^{15}\!/_{16}$ in. (58.4 x 73.5 cm.)

Isolated objects become reflections of the people who used them or worked with them, particularly when Wyeth painted the everyday environment and surroundings of Christina and Alvaro Olson at the Olson farm in Maine. Alvaro's egg scales, his ash basket full of blueberries and the blue bowl used to measure feed are such singular subjects. Geraniums on the windowsill, a rocking chair, and in this case, a teapot, symbolize Christina. "After Christina's death her cracked teapot sat as a reminder of a vanished elegance on the parlor mantle."

26. HAY LEDGE
1957. Egg tempera on panel.
21½ x 45¼ in. (54.6 x 114.9 cm.)

Alvaro Olson refused to pose for his friend, but Wyeth found a portrait of Alvaro resting on a hay ledge in the barn. "...he actually loved the sea, Alvaro, but I think to be near his sister, who needed him, he started this enormous truck garden. He kept that dory there, something that he loved, and it was there his whole life. And it was always painted white."

27. END OF OLSONS
1969. Egg tempera on panel.
18¾ x 19½ in. (47.6 x 49.5 cm.)

Wyeth returned to the house following the deaths of Christina and Alvaro Olson, and looking out an upper story window that is visible in *Weather Side*, painted one last picture. "It has a double meaning of course, it is the end of Olsons, the kitchen, but also it *is* the end of Olsons."

CATALOGUE

1. CIDER BARREL
1968. Drybrush watercolor on paper.
22 x 29 in. (55.9 x 73.6 cm.)

Signature: "Andrew Wyeth", lower right.
Provenance: With E. Coe Kerr Gallery, Inc., New York,
New York
Mr. and Mrs. Joseph E. Levine, New York,
New York
With Frank E. Fowler, Lookout Mountain,
Tennessee, and E. Coe Kerr Gallery,
Inc., New York, New York
Holly and Arthur Magill Collection,
Greenville, South Carolina
Exhibitions: Museum of Fine Arts, Boston, Massa-
chusetts, *Andrew Wyeth,* July 17-
September 6, 1970, p. 130, no. 89, illus.
Andrew Crispo Gallery, New York, New
York, *Ten Americans, Masters of
Watercolor,* 1974, no. 149, illus.
Metropolitan Museum of Art, New York,
New York, *Two Worlds of Andrew
Wyeth: Kuerners and Olsons,* October
16, 1976-February 6, 1977, p. 189,
no. 112, illus.

2. CANADA
1974. Watercolor on paper.
18 x 29 in. (45.7 x 73.7 cm.)

Signature: "Andrew Wyeth", lower right.
Provenance: With E. Coe Kerr Gallery, Inc., New York,
New York
Mr. and Mrs. Joseph E. Levine, New York,
New York
With Frank E. Fowler, Lookout Mountain,
Tennessee, and E. Coe Kerr Gallery,
Inc., New York, New York
Holly and Arthur Magill Collection,
Greenville, South Carolina
Exhibitions: Metropolitan Museum of Art, New York,
New York, *Two Worlds of Andrew
Wyeth: Kuerners and Olsons,* October
16, 1976-February 6, 1977, p. 192,
no. 127, illus.

3. STUDY FOR THE IDES OF MARCH
ca. 1975. Watercolor and pencil on paper.
14¾ x 23¾ in. (37.5 x 60.4 cm.)

Signature: "A. Wyeth", lower left.
Provenance: Mrs. Charles Bent, Cannan, New
Hampshire
With Nicholas Wyeth
Martin Kodner, St. Louis, Missouri
Sheldon Shapiro, St. Louis, Missouri
A.C.A. Galleries, Inc., New York,
New York
Holly and Arthur Magill Collection,
Greenville, South Carolina
Greenville County Museum of Art,
Greenville, South Carolina, Gift of
Holly and Arthur Magill, Accession
No. 1342

4. THE QUAKER
1975. Egg tempera on panel.
36¾ x 40⅜ in. (93.3 x 102.6 cm.)

Signature: "Andrew Wyeth", lower right.
Provenance: With Nicholas Wyeth
Mr. and Mrs. Joseph E. Levine, New York,
New York
With Frank E. Fowler, Lookout Mountain,
Tennessee, and E. Coe Kerr Gallery,
Inc., New York, New York
Holly and Arthur Magill Collection,
Greenville, South Carolina
Exhibitions: Metropolitan Museum of Art, New York,
New York, *Two Worlds of Andrew
Wyeth: Kuerners and Olsons,* October
16, 1976-Februry 6, 1977, p. 192,
no. 128, illus.

5. TOM'S SHED
1960. Watercolor on paper.
14 x 19⅞ in. (35.6 x 50.5 cm.)

Signature: "Andrew Wyeth", lower left.
Provenance: Marion S. Carson, Philadelphia,
Pennsylvania
Hammer Galleries, New York, New York
Mr. and Mrs. Joseph E. Levine,
New York, New York
With Frank E. Fowler, Lookout Mountain,
Tennessee, and E. Coe Kerr Gallery,
Inc., New York, New York
Holly and Arthur Magill Collection,
Greenville, South Carolina
Exhibitions: Metropolitan Museum of Art, New York,
New York, *Two Worlds of Andrew
Wyeth: Kuerners and Olsons*, October
16, 1976-February 6, 1977, p. 189,
no. 105, illus.

6. NOGEESHIK
1972. Egg tempera on panel.
24⅝ x 21¹⁵⁄₁₆ in. (62.5 x 55.7 cm.)

Signature: "AW", upper right.
Inscription: "By — Andrew Wyeth
NOGEESHIK AQUA," on back.
Remaining part of inscription is
obscured by wooden stretcher.
Provenance: With Nicholas Wyeth
Mr. and Mrs. Joseph E. Levine, New York,
New York
With Frank E. Fowler, Lookout Mountain,
Tennessee, and E. Coe Kerr Gallery,
Inc., New York, New York
Holly and Arthur Magill Collection,
Greenville, South Carolina
Exhibitions: M. H. de Young Museum, San Francisco,
California, *The Art of Andrew Wyeth,*
June 16-September 3, 1973, pp. 145,
147, 150, no. 90, illus.
Metropolitan Museum of Art, New York,
New York, *Two Worlds of Andrew
Wyeth: Kuerners and Olsons*, October
16, 1976-February 6, 1977, p. 38,
no. 31, illus.
Bibliography: *American Art Review,* Volume 1,
Number 1, p. 94, illus.

7. PETER WYETH HURD
1961. Drybrush watercolor and pencil on paper.
18 x 23¼ in. (45.7 x 59.1 cm.)

Signature: "Andrew Wyeth", upper right.
Provenance: With E. Coe Kerr Gallery, Inc., New
York, New York
Mr. and Mrs. Joseph E. Levine, New
York, New York
With Frank E. Fowler, Lookout Mountain,
Tennessee, and E. Coe Kerr Gallery,
Inc., New York, New York
Holly and Arthur Magill Collection,
Greenville, South Carolina
Exhibitions: Albright-Knox Art Gallery, Buffalo, New
York, *Andrew Wyeth Temperas,
Watercolors and Drawings*, November
2-December 9, 1962, pp. 16, 71,
no. 139, illus.
University of Arizona Art Gallery,
Tucson, Arizona, *Andrew Wyeth, An
Exhibition of Watercolors, Temperas
and Drawings*, March 16-April 14,
1963, p. 71, no. 90
Metropolitan Museum of Art, New York,
New York, *Two Worlds of Andrew
Wyeth: Kuerners and Olsons*, October
16, 1976-February 6, 1977, p. 189,
no. 106, illus.

8. FROM THE CAPES
1974. Egg tempera on panel.
24¼ x 18⅝ in. (61.6 x 47.3 cm.)

Signature: "Andrew Wyeth", upper right.
Provenance: With Nicholas Wyeth
Mr. and Jrs. Joseph E. Levine, New
York, New York
With Frank E. Fowler, Lookout Mountain,
Tennessee, and E. Coe Kerr Gallery,
Inc., New York, New York
Holly and Arthur Magill Collection,
Greenville, South Carolina
Exhibition: Metropolitan Museum of Art, New York,
New York, *Two Worlds of Andrew
Wyeth: Kuerners and Olsons*, October
16, 1976-February 6, 1977, p. 192,
no. 126, illus.

9. BUZZARD'S GLORY

1968. Egg tempera on panel.
18½ x 23⅜ in. (47 x 60.6 cm.)

Signature:	"Andrew Wyeth", upper left.
Provenance:	With E. Coe Kerr Gallery, Inc., New York, New York
	Mr. and Mrs. Joseph E. Levine, New York, New York
	With Frank E. Fowler, Lookout Mountain, Tennessee, and E. Coe Kerr Gllaery, Inc., New York, New York
	Holly and Arthur Magill Collection, Greenville, South Carolina
Exhibitions:	The White House, Washington, D.C., opened February 20, 1970, for an exhibition of one month duration.
	Museum of Fine Arts, Boston, Massachusetts, *Andrew Wyeth*, July 17-September 6, 1970, pp. 20, 47, no. 87, illus.
	Metropolitan Museum of Art, New York, New York, *Two Worlds of Andrew Wyeth: Kuerners and Olsons*, October 16, 1976-February 6, 1977, p. 189, no. 110, illus.

10. RAIN CLOUDS

1969. Watercolor on paper.
30¾ x 22 1/16 in. (78.1 x 56 cm.)

Signature:	"Andrew Wyeth", lower right.
Provenance:	With E. Coe Kerr Gallery, Inc., New York, New York
	Mr. and Mrs. Joseph E. Levine, New York, New York
	With Frank E. Fowler, Lookout Mountain, Tennessee, and E. Coe Kerr Gallery, Inc., New York, New York
	Holly and Arthur Magill Collection, Greenville, South Carolina
Exhibitions:	Metropolitan Museum of Art, New York, New York, *Two Worlds of Andrew Wyeth: Kuerners and Olsons*, October 16, 1976-February 6, 1977, p. 191, no. 120, illus.

11. THE SWINGER

1969. Drybrush watercolor on paper.
15⅜ x 25 11/16 in. (39.1 x 65.2 cm.) image

Signature:	"Andrew Wyeth", upper right.
Provenance:	With E. Coe Kerr Gallery, Inc., New York, New York
	Mr. and Mrs. Joseph E. Levine, New York, New York
	With Frank E. Fowler, Lookout Mountain, Tennessee, and E. Coe Kerr Gallery, Inc., New York, New York
	Holly and Arthur Magill Collection, Greenville, South Carolina
Exhibitions:	The White House, Washington, D.C., opened February 20, 1970 for an exhibition of one month duration.
	Museum of Fine Arts, Boston, Massachusetts, *Andrew Wyeth*, July 17-September 6, 1970, pp. 15, 136, no. 95, illus.
	Andrew Crispo Gallery, New York, New York, *Ten Americans, Masters of Watercolor*, 1974, no. 150, illus.
	Metropolitan Museum of Art, New York, New York, *Two Worlds of Andrew Wyeth: Kuerners and Olsons*, October 16, 1976-February 6, 1977, p. 191, no. 121, illus.

12. THE KASS

1978. Watercolor on paper.
22⅞ x 28⅞ in. (58.1 x 73.4 cm.)

Signature:	"Andrew Wyeth", upper left.
Provenance:	With Nicholas Wyeth
	Mr. and Mrs. Joseph E. Levine, New York, New York
	With Frank E. Fowler, Lookout Mountain, Tennessee, and E. Coe Kerr Gallery, Inc., New York, New York
	Holly and Arthur Magill Collection, Greenville, South Carolina

13. KITCHEN GARDEN
1962. Drybrush watercolor on paper.
23½ x 22¼ in. (59.7 x 56.5 cm.)

Signature: "Andrew Wyeth", lower left.
Verso: Rough preliminary sketch of head of Anna Kuerner in pencil, smudged.

Provenance: With M. Knoedler and Company, Inc., New York, New York
Mr. and Mrs. John T. Landreth, Lake Forest, Illinois
Mr. and Mrs. Joseph E. Levine, New York, New York
With Frank E. Fowler, Lookout Mountain, Tennessee, and E. Coe Kerr Gallery, Inc., New York, New York
Holly and Arthur Magill Collection, Greenville, South Carolina

Exhibitions: Albright-Knox Art Gallery, Buffalo, New York, *Andrew Wyeth Temperas, Watercolors and Drawings*, November 2-December 9, 1962, p. 16, 75, no. 143, illus.
Pennsylvania Academy of the Fine Arts, Philadelphia, Pennsylvania, *One Hundred and Fifty-Eighth Annual Exhibition/Watercolors, Prints, Drawings*, January 18-March 3, 1963, no. 480.
University of Arizona Art Gallery, Tucson, Arizona, *Andrew Wyeth, An Exhibition of Watercolors, Temperas, and Drawings*, March 16-April 14, 1963, p. 71, no. 92.
Pennsylvania Academy of the Fine Arts, Philadelphia, Pennsylvania, *Andrew Wyeth*, October 5-November 27, 1966, p. 84, no. 175.

Also traveled to:
Baltimore Museum of Art, Baltimore, Maryland, December 11, 1966-January 22, 1967.
Whitney Museum of American Art, New York, New York, February 6-April 12, 1967.
The Art Institute of Chicago, Chicago, Illinois, April 21-June 4, 1967.
Oklahoma Museum of Art, Oklahoma City, Oklahoma, *Andrew Wyeth*, December 3-24, 1967, p. 22, no. 17, illus.
Metropolitan Museum of Art, New York, New York, *Two Worlds of Andrew Wyeth: Kuerners and Olsons*, October 16, 1976-February 6, 1977, p. 189, no. 107, illus.

Bibliography: Betsy James Wyeth, *Wyeth at Kuerners*, (Boston: Houghton Mifflin and Company, 1976), p. 156, illus.

14. LODEN COAT

1978. Watercolor on paper.

30 x 22 in. (76.2 x 55.9 cm.)

Signature: "Andrew Wyeth", lower left.

Provenance: With Nicholas Wyeth
Mr. and Mrs. Joseph E. Levine, New
York, New York
With Frank E. Fowler, Lookout
Mountain, Tennessee, and E. Coe
Kerr Gallery, Inc., New York, New York
Holly and Arthur Magill Collection,
Greenville, South Carolina

15. FENCE LINE

1967. Watercolor on paper.

21⅞ x 30 in. (55.6 x 76.2 cm.)

Signature: "Andrew Wyeth", lower left.

Provenance: Mr. Imre Rosenthal, New York, New York
Gallery Master, Ltd., New York, New York
Mr. and Mrs. Joseph E. Levine, New
York, New York
With Frank E. Fowler, Lookout
Mountain, Tennessee, and E. Coe Kerr
Gallery, Inc., New York, New York
Holly and Arthur Magill Collection,
Greenville, South Carolina

Exhibitions: Museum of Fine Arts, Boston,
Massachusetts, *Andrew Wyeth*,
July 17-September 6, 1970, p. 121,
no. 75, illus.
Metropolitan Museum of Art, New York,
New York, *Two Worlds of Andrew
Wyeth: Kuerners and Olsons,*
October 16, 1976-February 6, 1977,
p. 22, no. 18, illus.

Bibliography: Betsy James Wyeth, *Wyeth at Kuerners*,
(Boston: Houghton Mifflin and
Company, 1976), p. 67, illus.

16. RUM RUNNER (STUDY OF WALTER ANDERSON)

1974. Watercolor on paper.

15 x 8 in. (38.1 x 20.3 cm.)

Signature: "A. Wyeth", center left.

Provenance: Mr. and Mrs. Joseph E. Levine, New
York, New York
With Frank E. Fowler, Lookout
Mountain, Tennessee, and E. Coe
Kerr Gallery, Inc., New York, New York
Holly and Arthur Magill Collection,
Greenville, South Carolina

Exhibitions: Metropolitan Museum of Art, New York,
New York, *Two Worlds of Andrew
Wyeth: Kuerners and Olsons,*
October 16, 1976-February 6, 1977,
p. 188, no. 100, illus.

17. RUM RUNNER*

1944-1974. Egg tempera on panel.
25 x 48 in. (63.5 x 121.9 cm.)

Signature: "Andrew Wyeth", lower right.
Provenance: Mr. and Mrs. Frank Webster, Medfield, Massachusetts
With Doll & Richards, Boston, Massachusetts
With Sotheby Parke Bernet, Inc., New York, New York
E. Coe Kerr Gallery, Inc., New York, New York
Mr. and Mrs. Joseph E. Levine, New York, New York
With Frank E. Fowler, Lookout Mountain, Tennessee, and E. Coe Kerr Gallery, Inc., New York, New York
Holly and Arthur Magill Collection, Greenville, South Carolina
Exhibitions: Metropolitan Museum of Art, New York, New York, *Two Worlds of Andrew Wyeth: Kuerners and Olsons,* October 16, 1976-February 6, 1977, p. 188, no. 100, illus.

18. SEA SNAILS

1953. Watercolor on paper.
20 x 28⅛ in. (50.8 x 71.4 cm.)

Signature: "Andrew Wyeth", lower left.
Provenance: With M. Knoedler and Company, Inc., New York, New York
Mr. and Mrs. Joseph E. Levine, New York, New York
With Frank E. Fowler, Lookout Mountain, Tennessee, and E. Coe Kerr Gallery, Inc., New York, New York
Holly and Arthur Magill Collection, Greenville, South Carolina
Exhibitions: Oklahoma Museum of Art, Oklahoma City, Oklahoma, *The Wonder of Andrew Wyeth,* December 3-24, 1967, p. 22, no. 17, illus.
Metropolitan Museum of Art, New York, New York, *Two Worlds of Andrew Wyeth: Kuerners and Olsons,* October 16, 1976-February 6, 1977, p. 188, no. 101, illus.

*Originally painted in 1944 and entitled *To The Westward,* the subject was Andrew Wyeth's friend Walter Anderson from Port Clyde, Maine. The subject is standing by a beached dory. The tempera was purchased by E. Coe Kerr Gallery on May 16, 1973 at an auction at Sotheby Parke Bernet, Inc., New York, New York (Sale No. 3520, Lot No. 178). In the fall of 1973 the painting was loaned to an exhibition in Oklahoma City, Oklahoma, a benefit for the Young Presidents Association annual meeting. The painting was badly damaged in the return shipment, and subsequently forwarded to Andrew Wyeth for repair. After discussion with E. Coe Kerr Gallery, the artist chose to repaint his friend Walter Anderson, and add the sails of a mystical rum runner's boat, visible above the dunes in the upper left quadrant of the painting. The work was completed by the artist in 1974 and retitled *Rum Runner.*

19. TEEL'S ISLAND
1954. Drybrush watercolor on paper.
10 x 23 in. (25.4 x 58.4 cm.)

Signature: "Andrew Wyeth", lower left.
Provenance: With Mr. Knoedler and Company, Inc.
New York, New York
Mr. and Mrs. Robert Montgomery,
New York, New York
Wildenstein and Company, New York,
New York
Mr. and Mrs. Joseph E. Levine, New
York, New York
With Frank E. Fowler, Lookout
Mountain, Tennessee, and E. Coe
Kerr Gallery, Inc., New York,
New York
Holly and Arthur Magill Collection,
Greenville, South Carolina

Exhibitions: Ogunquit Museum of Art, Ogunquit,
Maine, *American of Our Times and
Andrew Wyeth*, Third Annual Exhibi-
tion, July 1-September 11, 1955,
no. 14, illus.
M. Knoedler and Company, Inc., New
York, New York, *Andrew Wyeth:
Recent Paintings*, October 28-
November 22, 1958, no. 38, illus.
Albright-Knox Art Gallery, Buffalo,
New York, *Andrew Wyeth Temperas,
Watercolors and Drawings*,
November 2-December 9, 1962,
p. 14, opposite p. 60, no. 111, illus.
Fogg Art Museum, Harvard University,
Cambridge, Massachusetts, *Andrew
Wyeth: Drybrush and Pencil
Drawings*, January 15-February 28,
1963, no. 25, illus.
Also traveled to:
The Pierpont Morgan Library, New
York, New York, March 14-
April 27, 1963.
The Corcoran Gallery of Art,
Washington, D.C., May 16-June 16,
1963.
William A. Farnsworth Library and
Art Museum, Rockland, Maine,
July 18-September 2, 1963.

Pennsylvania Academy of the Fine Arts,
Philadelphia, Pennsylvania, *Andrew
Wyeth*, October 5-November 27,
1966, pp. 50-51, no. 77, illus.
Also traveled to:
Baltimore Museum of Art, Baltimore,
Maryland, December 11, 1966-
January 22, 1967.
Whitney Museum of American Art,
New York, New York, February 6-
April 12, 1967.
The Art Institute of Chicago, Chicago,
Illinois, April 21-June 4, 1967.
The White House, Washington, D.C.,
opened February 20, 1970 for an
exhibition of one month duration.
Museum of Fine Arts, Boston,
Massachusetts, *Andrew Wyeth*,
July 17-September 6, 1970, p. 176,
no. 114, illus.
Andrew Crispo Gallery, New York,
New York, *Ten Americans, Masters
of Watercolor*, 1974, no. 144, illus.
Metropolitan Museum of Art, New
York, New York, *Two Worlds of
Andrew Wyeth: Kuerners and Olsons*,
October 16, 1976-February 6, 1977,
p. 188, no. 103, illus.

Bibliography: Lloyd Goodrich, "Andrew Wyeth," *Art
in America*, (October, 1955), p. 22,
illus.
Lloyd Goodrich, "Four Seasons, Dry-
brush Drawings by Andrew Wyeth,"
Art in America, (Summer, 1962),
p. 41, illus.
Roul Tunley, "Artist at Home," *Woman's
Day*, (August, 1963), p. 36, illus.
A. Mongan, "Drawings of Andrew
Wyeth," *American Artist*, (September,
1963), pp. 31, 74, illus.
J. Jacobs, "Andrew Wyeth, An
Unsentimental Reappraisal," *Art in
America*, (January, 1967), p. 28,
illus.
Richard Meryman, *Andrew Wyeth*,
(Boston: Houghton Mifflin Company,
1968), p. 154, illus.
Art in America, (May, 1974), p. 7, illus.

20. ELWELL'S SAWMILL

1968. Watercolor on paper.
22 1/16 x 30 5/8 in. (56 x 77.8 cm.)

Signature: "Andrew Wyeth", lower right.

Provenance: With M. Knoedler and Company, Inc., New York, New York

Mr. and Mrs. Joseph E. Levine, New York, New York

With Frank E. Fowler, Lookout Mountain, Tennessee, and E. Coe Kerr Gallery, Inc., New York, New York

Holly and Arthur Magill Collection, Greenville, South Carolina

Exhibitions: Museum of Fine Arts, Boston, Massachusetts, *Andrew Wyeth,* July 17-September 6, 1970, p. 219, no. 162, illus.

Metropolitan Museum of Art, New York, New York, *Two Worlds of Andrew Wyeth: Kuerners and Olsons,* October 16, 1976-February 6, 1977, p. 190, no. 113, illus.

21. LOGGING SCOOT

1968. Watercolor on paper.
22 x 30 1/2 in. (55.9 x 77.5 cm.)

Signature: "Andrew Wyeth", lower right.

Provenance: With M. Knoedler and Company, Inc., New York, New York

Mr. and Mrs. Joseph E. Levine, New York, New York

With Frank E. Fowler, Lookout Mountain, Tennessee, and E. Coe Kerr Gallery, Inc., New York, New York

Holly and Arthur Magill Collection, Greenville, South Carolina

Exhibitions: Museum of Fine Arts, Boston, Massachusetts, *Andrew Wyeth,* July 17-September 6, 1970, p. 220, no. 163, illus.

Metropolitan Museum of Art, New York, New York, *Two Worlds of Andrew Wyeth: Kuerners and Olsons,* October 16, 1976-February 6, 1977, p. 190, no. 114, illus.

22. SPRUCE BOUGH

1969. Watercolor on paper.
21¾ x 29¹⁵⁄₁₆ in. (55.2 x 76 cm.)

Signature: "Andrew Wyeth", upper left.

Provenance: With Nicholas Wyeth, Inc., New York, New York

Mr. and Mrs. Joseph E. Levine, New York, New York

With Frank E. Fowler, Lookout Mountain, Tennessee, and E. Coe Kerr Gallery, Inc., New York, New York

Holly and Arthur Magill Collection, Greenville, South Carolina

Exhibitions: The White House, Washington, D.C. opened February 20, 1970 for an exhibition of one month duration.

Museum of Fine Arts, Boston, Massachusetts, *Andrew Wyeth*, July 17-September 6, 1970, pp. 164-165, no. 170, illus.

Metropolitan Museum of Art, New York, New York, *Two Worlds of Andrew Wyeth: Kuerners and Olsons*, October 16, 1976-February 6, 1977, p. 190, no. 118, illus.

23. THE FINN

1969. Drybrush watercolor on paper.
29¾ x 21½ in. (75.5 x 54.6 cm.)

Signature: "Andrew Wyeth", lower left.

Provenance: With Nicholas Wyeth, Inc., New York, New York

Mr. and Mrs. Joseph E. Levine, New York, New York

With Frank E. Fowler, Lookout Mountain, Tennessee, and E. Coe Kerr Gallery, Inc., New York, New York

Holly and Arthur Magill Collection, Greenville, South Carolina

Exhibitions: The White House, Washington, D.C., opened February 20, 1970 for an exhibition of one month duration.

Museum of Fine Arts, Boston, Massachusetts, *Andrew Wyeth*, July 17-September 6, 1970, pp. 24, 162-163, no. 169, illus.

Andrew Crispo Gallery, New York, New York, *Ten Americans, Masters of Watercolor*, 1974, no. 152, illus.

Metropolitan Museum of Art, New York, New York, *Two Worlds of Andrew Wyeth: Kuerners and Olsons*, October 16, 1976-February 6, 1977, p. 172, no. 182, illus.

Bibliography: D. Davis, "World of Wyeth: Exhibition in Boston," *Newsweek*, (August 24, 1970), pp. 55-56, illus.

Wanda M. Corn, *The Art of Andrew Wyeth*, (Greenwich, Connecticut: New York Graphic Society, Ltd., 1973), pp. 103, 147, illus.

R. Hughes, "Wyeth's Cold Comfort: Exhibition at the Metropolitan Museum," *Time*, November 1, 1976), p. 69, illus.

24. WEATHER SIDE

1965. Egg tempera on panel.
48⅛ x 27⅞ in. (122.2 x 70.8 cm.)

Signature: "Andrew Wyeth", lower left.
Inscription: "WEATHER SIDE
CUSHING 1965," on back.
Provenance: With M. Knoedler and Company, Inc.,
New York, New York
Mr. and Mrs. Alexander M. Laughlin,
New York, New York
E. Coe Kerr Gallery, Inc., New York
New York
Mr. and Mrs. Joseph E. Levine, New
York, New York
With Frank E. Fowler, Lookout Mountain,
Tennessee, and E. Coe Kerr Gallery,
Inc., New York, New York
Holly and Arthur Magill Collection,
Greenville, South Carolina
Exhibitions: Pennsylvania Academy of the Fine Arts,
Philadelphia, Pennsylvania, *Andrew
Wyeth,* October 5-November 27, 1966,
pp. 102-103, no. 217, illus.
Also traveled to:
Baltimore Museum of Art, Baltimore,
Maryland, December 11, 1966-
January 22, 1967.
Whitney Museum of American Art,
New York, New York, February 6-
April 12, 1967.
The Art Institute of Chicago, Chicago,
Illinois, April 21-June 4, 1967.

Museum of Fine Arts, Boston
Massachusetts, *Andrew Wyeth,* July
17-September 6, 1970, pp. 21, 207,
no. 148, illus.
M. H. de Young Museum, San Francisco,
California, *The Art of Andrew Wyeth,*
June 16-September 3, 1973, pp. 106,
158-159, no. 66, illus.
The National Museum of Modern Art,
Tokyo, Tokyo, Japan, *Works of
Andrew Wyeth, Japan,* April 6-May
19, 1974, no. 52.
Also traveled to:
The National Museum of Modern Art,
Kyoto, Kyoto, Japan, June and July,
1974.
Metropolitan Museum of Art, New York,
New York, *Two Worlds of Andrew
Wyeth: Kuerners and Olsons,* October
16, 1976-February 6, 1977, pp. 150,
152-154, 157-158, no. 156, illus.
Bibliography: "Exhibit at Whitney Museum," *Arts,*
(March, 1967), p. 54, illus.
"Wyeth's World," *Newsweek,* (March,
1967), pp. 76-78, illus.
John Canaday, "A Doubleheader Down
East," *The New York Times,* (August
1, 1971), Section II, p. 17, illus.
A. Werner, "Before the Squalor (The
Native Landscape as Viewed by
American 19th and 20th Century
Painters)," *Art and Artists,* (February,
1977), p. 12, illus.

25. CHRISTINA'S TEAPOT
1968. Watercolor on paper.
23 x 28¹⁵⁄₁₆ in. (58.4 x 73.5 cm.)

Signature: "Andrew Wyeth", upper right.
Provenance: With M. Knoedler and Company, Inc.,
             New York, New York
             Mr. and Mrs. Joseph E. Levine, New
             York, New York
             With Frank E. Fowler, Lookout Mountain,
             Tennessee, and E. Coe Kerr Gallery,
             Inc., New York, New York
             Holly and Arthur Magill Collection,
             Greenville, South Carolina
Exhibitions: Oklahoma Museum of Art, Oklahoma
             City, Oklahoma, *Andrew Wyeth*,
             December 3-24, 1967, p. 22, no.
             17, illus.
             Krannert Art Museum, University of
             Illinois, Urbana, Illinois, *Contemporary
             American Painting and Sculpture*,
             April, 1969.
             Metropolitan Museum of Art, New York,
             New York, *Two Worlds of Andrew
             Wyeth: Kuerners and Olsons*, October
             16, 1976-February 6, 1977, p. 189,
             no. 111, illus.

26. HAY LEDGE
1957. Egg tempera on panel.
21½ x 45¼ in. (54.6 x 114.9 cm.)

Signature: "Andrew Wyeth", lower left.
Provenance: Mrs. John Carmack, New York,
             New York
             With E. Coe Kerr Gallery, Inc., New
             York, New York
             Mr. and Mrs. Joseph E. Levine, New
             York, New York
             With Frank E. Fowler, Lookout Mountain,
             Tennessee, and E. Coe Kerr Gallery,
             Inc., New York, New York
             Holly and Arthur Magill Collection,
             Greenville, South Carolina
Exhibitions: M. Knoedler and Company, New York,
             New York, *Andrew Wyeth: Recent
             Paintings*, October 28-November 22,
             1958, no. 35, illus.

University of Arizona Art Gallery,
Tucson, Arizona, *Andrew Wyeth, An
Exhibition of Watercolors, Temperas
and Drawings*, March 16-April 14,
1963, pp. 68, 89, no. 63, illus.
Pennsylvania Academy of the Fine Arts,
Philadelphia, Pennsylvania, *Andrew
Wyeth*, October 5-November 27, 1966,
p. 61, no. 109, illus.
Also traveled to:
Baltimore Museum of Art, Baltimore,
Maryland, December 11, 1966-
January 22, 1967.
Whitney Museum of American Art,
New York, New York, February 6-
April 12, 1967.
The Art Institute of Chicago, Chicago,
Illinois, April 21-June 4, 1967.
The White House, Washington, D.C.,
opened February 20, 1970, for an
exhibition of one month duration.
Museum of Fine Arts, Boston,
Massachusetts, *Andrew Wyeth*, July
17-September 6, 1970, p. 183, no.
121, illus.
Metropolitan Museum of Art, New York,
New York, *Two Worlds of Andrew
Wyeth: Kuerners and Olsons*, October
16, 1976-February 6, 1977, pp. 158,
162-163, 165, no. 170, illus.

Bibliography: H. C. Pitz, "Andrew Wyeth," *American
             Artist*, (November, 1958), p. 30, illus.
             Richard Meryman, *Andrew Wyeth*,
             (Boston: Houghton Mifflin Company,
             1968), pp. 244-245, illus.
             Wanda M. Corn, *The Art of Andrew
             Wyeth*, (Greenwich, Connecticut:
             New York Graphic Society Ltd.,
             1973), pp. 27, 31, illus.
             C. Roy, "Andrew Wyeth," *Connaissance
             Des Arts*, (November, 1976), p. 58,
             illus.
             Brian O'Doherty, *American Masters:
             The Voice and the Myth*, (New York:
             Random House, 1977), p. 111, illus.

27. END OF OLSONS
1969. Egg tempera on panel.
18¾ x 19½ in. (47.6 x 49.5 cm.)

Signature: "A.W.", ⅞" (2.2 cm.) from bottom edge and 5⅜" (13.6 cm.) from right edge, located in shingles of house.

Provenance: With E. Coe Kerr Gallery, Inc., New York, New York
Mr. and Mrs. Joseph E. Levine, New York, New York
With Frank E. Fowler, Lookout Mountain, Tennessee, and E. Coe Kerr Gallery, Inc., New York, New York
Holly and Arthur Magill Collection, Greenville, South Carolina

Exhibitions: Museum of Fine Arts, Boston, Massachusetts, *Andrew Wyeth*, July 17-September 6, 1970, pp. 160-161, no. 168, illus.
Metropolitan Museum of Art, New York, New York, *Two Worlds of Andrew Wyeth: Kuerners and Olsons*, October 16, 1976-February 6, 1977, pp. 158, 160, no. 165, illus.

Bibliography: D. David, "World of Wyeth: Exhibition in Boston," *Newsweek*, (August 24, 1970), p. 56, illus.
Wanda M. Corn, *The Art of Andrew Wyeth*, (Greenwich, Connecticut: New York Graphic Society Ltd., 1973), pp. 41, 43, 109, 152, illus.
K. Larson, "Andrew Wyeth, Monotone in a Minor Key." *Art News*, (December, 1976), p. 44, illus.

CATALOGUE

Catalogue design and photography by Blake Praytor. Color separations were prepared by Sterling Breeden of Graphic South, Charlotte, North Carolina, from transparencies made from the original artwork. Press proofs were compared to the original drybrush, watercolor and tempera paintings. Type is Americana and American Gothic, set by the Typography Shop, Atlanta, Georgia. The catalogue was printed on a two color Miehle offset press by Albert Williams of Keys Printing Company, Greenville, South Carolina. Cover and text paper is Cameo Dull manufactured by S. D. Warren Company, a division of Scott Paper Company. End sheets are Rhododendron Pryo Brown manufactured by Strathmore Paper Company. Cover fabric for case bound catalogue is Brown Roxite produced by Holliston Mills, Lincoln, Rhode Island. Case binding was performed by Carolina Ruling and Binding, Charlotte, North Carolina.